I0605752

My First BIG Book of PETS AND PET CARE

by Belinda Gallagher

Ruby Tuesday Books

Note from the Publisher
Neither the publisher nor the author can accept legal responsibility or liability for any loss, harm, or injury that may come about from following the instructions, guidance, or information in this book. All pet care should be undertaken with guidance from a pet store or veterinarian and all pet care activities should be carried out with the guidance and supervision of an adult.

Published in 2026 by Ruby Tuesday Books Ltd.

Copyright © 2026 Ruby Tuesday Books Ltd.

All rights reserved. No part of this publication may be reproduced in whole or in part, stored in any retrieval system, or transmitted in any form or by any means, electronic, mechanical, photocopying, recording, or otherwise, without written permission from the publisher.

Editors: Ruth Owen & Mark J. Sachner
Design & Production: Alix Wood

Photo credits: Alamy: 17B (Juniors Bildarchiv GmbH), 67T (Jeffrey Isaac Greenberg), 72T (Juniors Bildarchiv GmbH), 73T (ImageBroker.com), 85T (Juniors Bildarchiv GmbH); Shutterstock: Cover (E LLL/Rita Kochmarjova/dien), 1 (Westock Productions), 4T (Monkey Business Images), 4B (Vasyl Syniuk), 5T (AYO Production), 5C, 6–7, 8T, 8CL (StockImageFactory.com), 8CR, 9, 10, 11T (Bear Fotos), 11B (SpeedKingz), 12T, 13TL (New Africa), 13TR (Monkey Business Images), 13B (Sangiao Photography), 14T (O. Kalacheva), 14B, 15T (Leszek Glasner), 15B, 16T (pirita), 17T, 17C (stockfour), 18 (Pressmaster), 19, 20T (Rido), 20B (Anton Gvozdikov), 21, 22T (Pixel-Shot), 22B (alexei-tm), 23T (wavebreakmedia), 23C (Pixel-Shot), 24–25, 26–27, 28–29, 30–31, 32–33, 34T (Anurak Pongpatimet), 34B, 35, 36–37, 38T, 38CR (Slaystorm), 38B, 39, 40, 41T (Garna Zarina), 41B, 42–43, 44–45, 46T (Southworks), 46B (Soloviova Liudmyla), 47T (Maria Moroz), 47B, 48–49, 50T (NDAB Creativity), 51T, 51B (evrymmnt), 52–53, 54–55, 56–57, 58–59, 60–61, 62T (New Africa), 62B, 63, 64–65, 66, 67B, 68–69, 70–71, 72B, 73C, 73B (The Image Party), 74–75, 76, 77T, 77BL (Lordn), 77BR, 78T, 78B (BestPhotoStudio), 79, 80–81, 82–83, 84T, 84B (Ruslana Iurchenko), 85B, 86, 87T, 88T, 89T, 89B (Zivica Kerkez), 90–91, 93, 94 (for a full detailed list of contributors, contact info@rubytuesdaybooks.com); Superstock: 87B (Heidi & Hans-Juergen Koch), 88B (Juniors Bildarchiv).

Library of Congress Control Number: 2025946370

Print (Hardback) ISBN 978-1-78856-636-0
Print (Paperback) ISBN 978-1-78856-637-7
ePub ISBN 978-1-78856-638-4

Published in Minneapolis, MN
Printed in the United States

www.rubytuesdaybooks.com

What's Inside?

Why Do We Keep Pets?

People love to keep pets!

Our pets make us happy, keep us healthy, and teach us how to be caring.

Pets become part of the family.

Pets love their owners, too.

They need people to care for them and provide food and a safe place to live.

Some pets are smart and enjoy learning.

We can teach them good manners, how to behave, and tricks!

Have People Always Kept Pets?

Yes! Thousands of years ago, people tamed wild wolves.

These first dogs helped people hunt, protected farm animals, and guarded homes.

Foxes, wolves, and pet dogs are all part of the same animal family.

Red fox

Gray wolf

Pekingese dog

Wild horses were tamed to help people travel long distances, and pull carts and farm machinery.

Zebras, wild horses, and pet ponies are all relatives.

Zebra

Wild horse

Pet Shetland pony

The **ancient Egyptians** kept African wildcats to hunt rats and mice that stole people's food.

The ancient Egyptians even made cat statues!

African wildcat

Over time, the wildcats became tame, much-loved pets.

Pet kitten

The cat family includes pet cats, wildcats, and the biggest cat of all—the tiger.

Can I Choose a Pet?

Yes, you can! But here are some things to talk about before your family decides which pet is best for you.

PET OR NO PET?

1. Why do we want a pet?
2. Do we have time?
3. Do we have space?
4. Who will help out?
5. How much will it cost?

Hamster in a toy wheel

If you don't have space for a larger pet, choose a small pet, such as a hamster that lives indoors.

A hamster will be awake at night. It may squeak, dig, run in its wheel, and make other noises!

Rabbits and guinea pigs get lonely.

Guinea pig

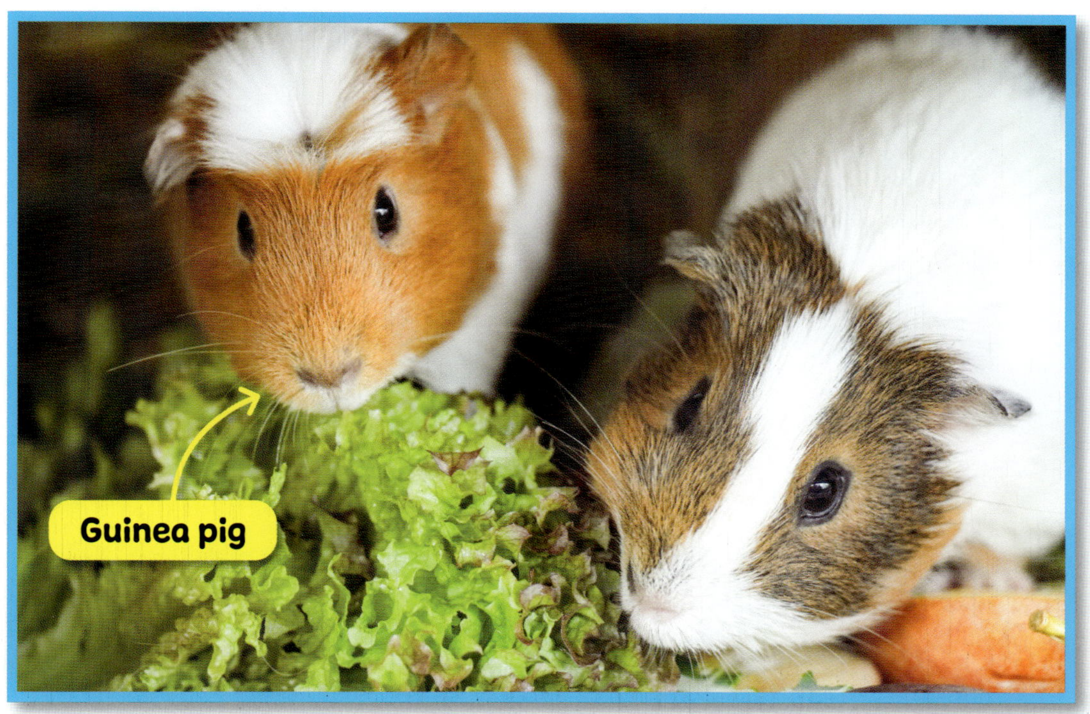

They need to live with others of their kind to be happy and healthy.

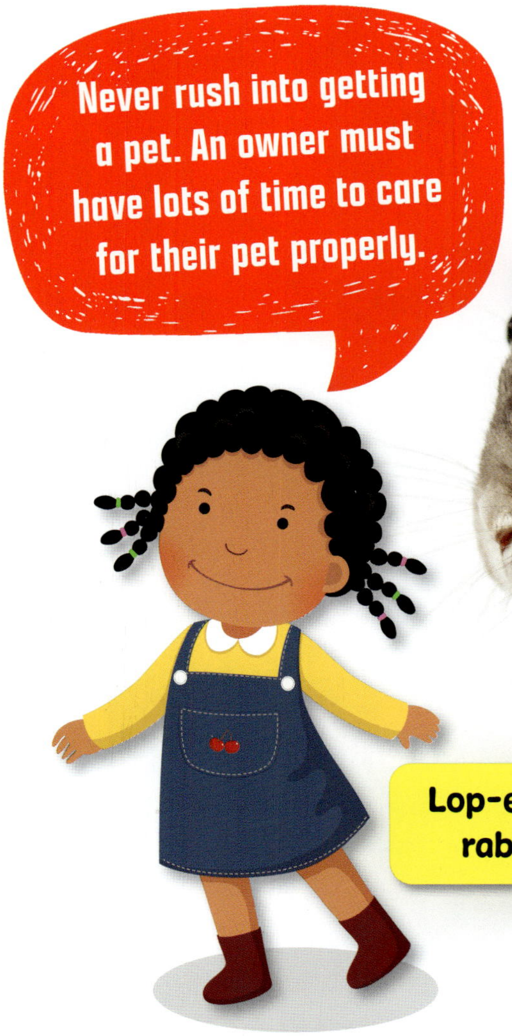
Never rush into getting a pet. An owner must have lots of time to care for their pet properly.

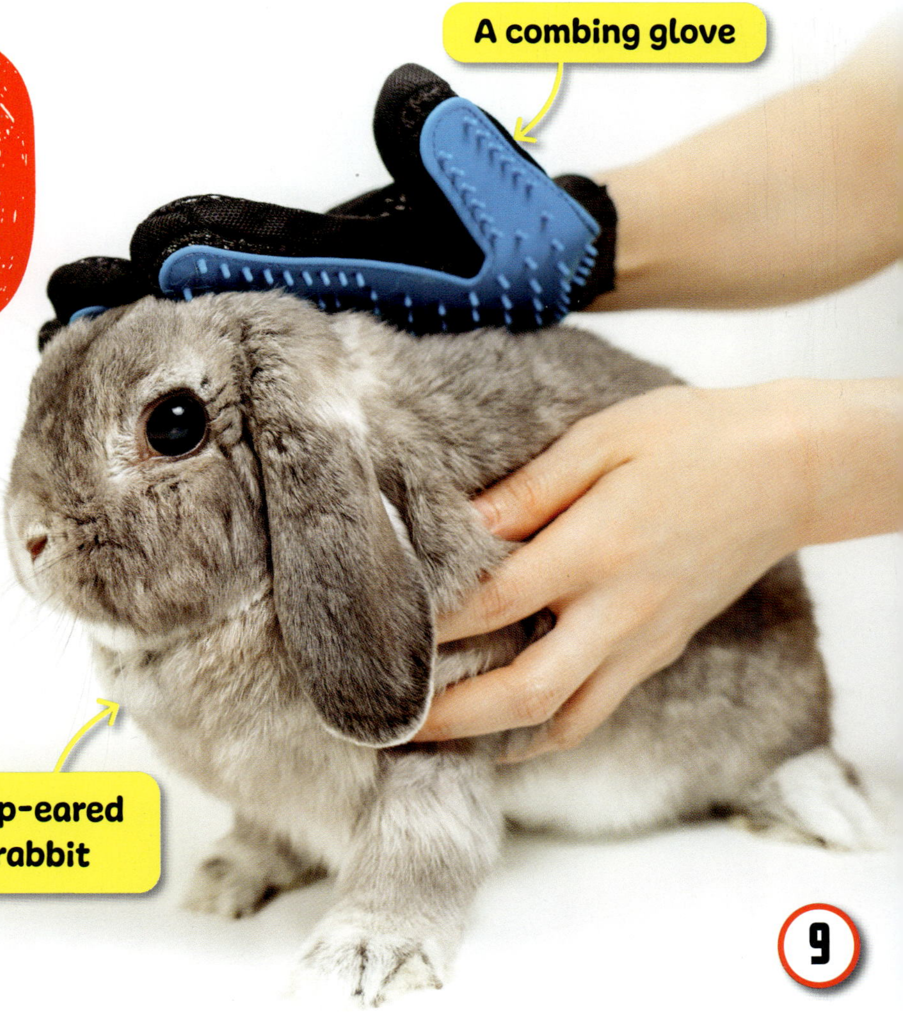
A combing glove
Lop-eared rabbit

Where Can I Get My New Pet?

Once you know the kind of pet you can care for, it's time to find one!

Many pets in **animal shelters** need a loving forever home.

Always start your search to find a pet by visiting animal shelters with your family.

The animal care workers at a shelter will help you choose a pet that best suits you.

A pet store can be a good place to look for smaller pets.

This girl is choosing a pet fish.

What if I Can't Have a Pet?

You may not be able to give a pet a home. But there are still plenty of ways you can care for animals.

If you have an outdoor space, feed the birds.

You can leave out a dish of water for wild animals.

Red squirrel

Watch from a window to see who visits.

Ask if you can help a friend by walking or grooming their dog.

You could help with feeding a friend's pet or cleaning its cage, too.

Visit an **animal sanctuary**.

These are safe, special places where rescued animals live for the rest of their lives.

Can I Pet an Alpaca?

Yes! You may not have space to keep an alpaca or llama.

However, you can visit a farm or animal sanctuary where you can pet them.

Always be quiet and gentle around all animals.

Alpacas and llamas are relatives of camels!

You might also meet goats and see baby animals at a farm.

Sometimes you are allowed to help feed the animals.

Only visit farms that take good care of their animals. Most do, but sadly not all.

Ask your grown-ups to help you check out a farm online before visiting.

Could I Care for a Pony?

Pet ponies are great fun, but also hard work!

If you want to learn pony care and riding, visit a pony club or riding school near you.

Always do pony care and riding with a grown-up close by.

At a pony club, you may be able to help fill a pony's hay net.

Hay net

Ponies love to eat hay.

You might help with grooming to keep a pony's coat free from dirt.

You could help sweep up dirty straw bedding from the stable floors.

You might even use a special shovel or scoop to pick up pony poop from the paddocks!

What if My Pet Gets Sick?

Just like people, pets can get sick.

When this happens, it's time to visit an animal doctor called a vet.

The vet may give your pet a shot or medicine to make it better.

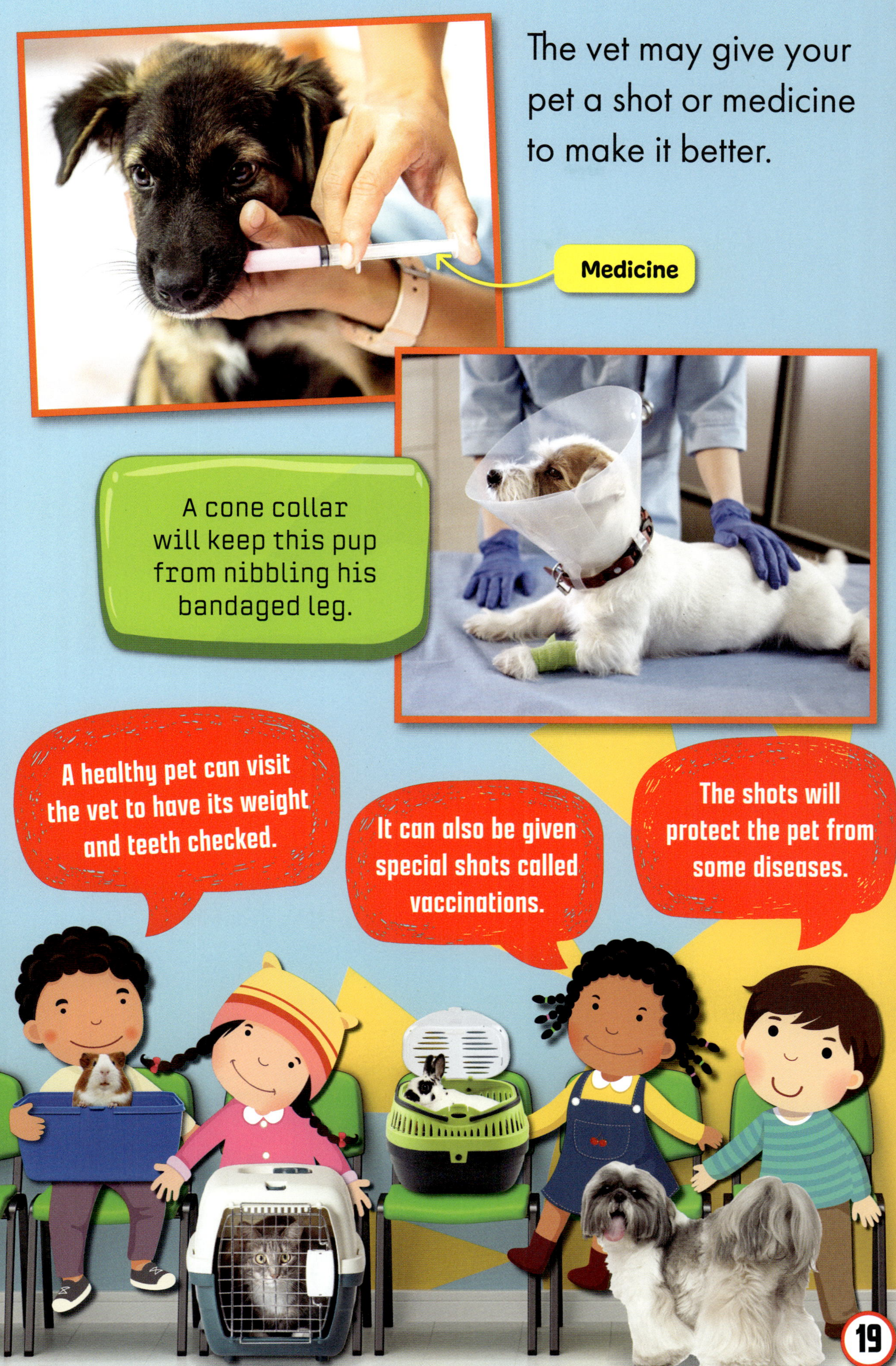

Who Helps Us Take Care of Our Pets?

Lots of caring people help us keep our pets happy!

When you go on vacation, your pet can't always go, too.

A pet sitter can visit your home to feed your pet.

Your dog may need a haircut, bath, and blow-dry!

Groomers keep dogs, cats, and other pets neat and clean.

Dog trainers can help us teach our dogs to be well-behaved.

This little puppy is being trained to walk on a leash.

When everyone is at school or work, a dog walker can collect your dog for a fun run around!

How Do Pets Help People?

Spending time around pets is good for us!

Scientists say that simply stroking a pet can help us feel calm and happy.

Playing games with our pets is fun for us and them.

It makes us feel good when our pets are happy to see us.

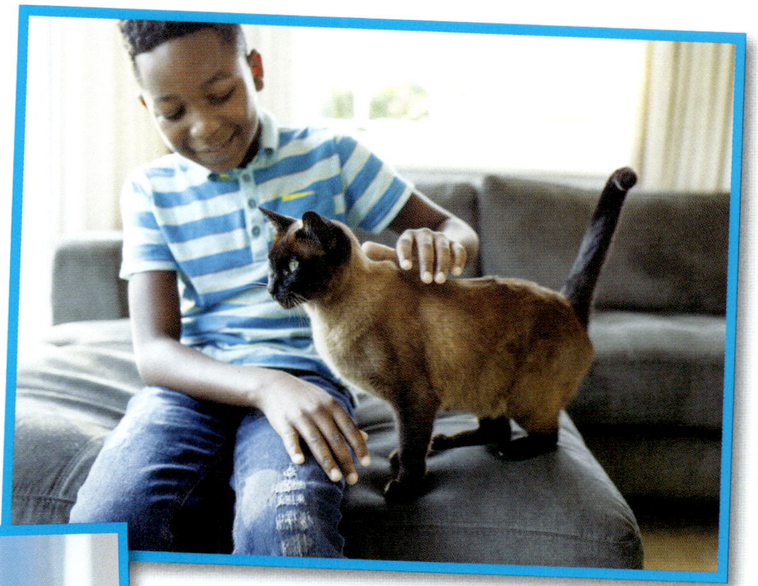

Pets teach us to be **responsible**.

Feeding a pet fish

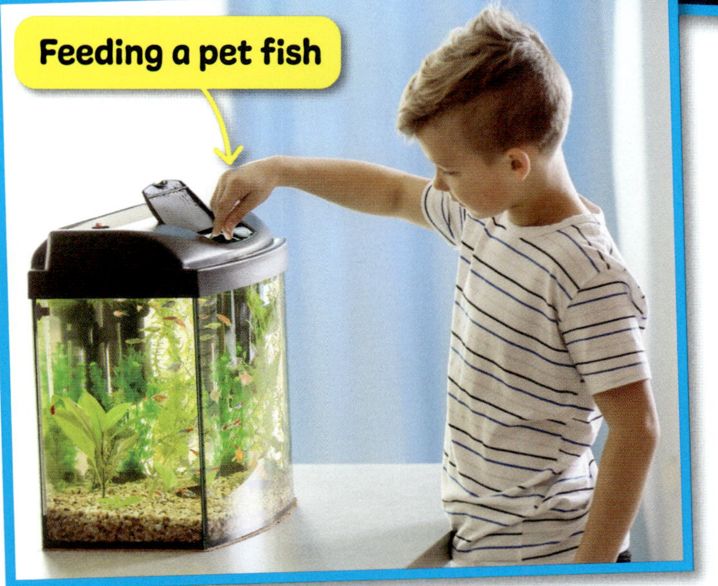

Jobs like cleaning a cage, feeding a pet, or picking up our dog's poop show we can put others first.

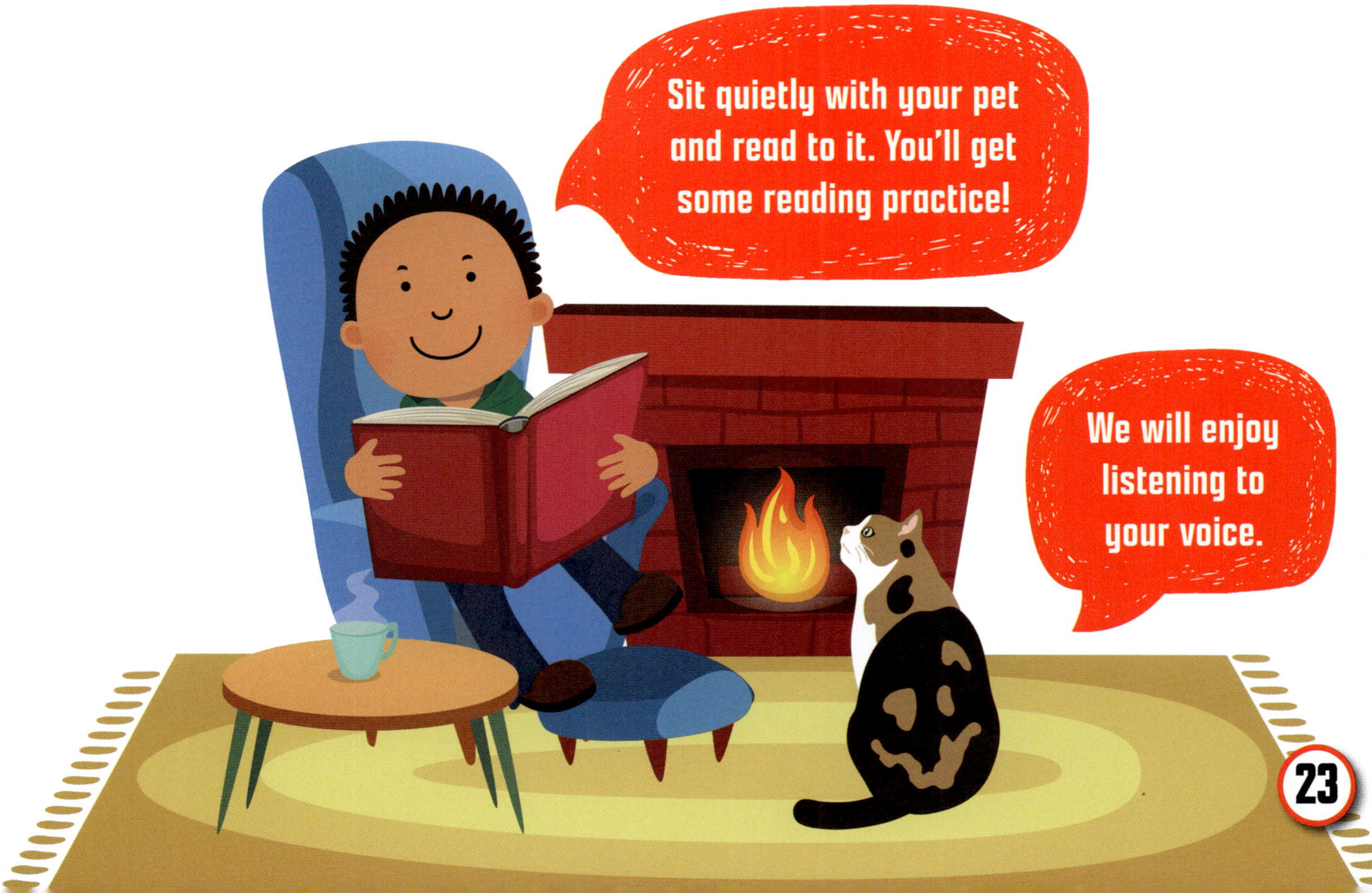
Sit quietly with your pet and read to it. You'll get some reading practice!
We will enjoy listening to your voice.

Why Do Cats Make Great Pets?

Cats are super pets!

Long tail

Soft fur

Whiskers

They are easy to care for, they enjoy playing, and they give lots of love back to their owners.

Pet cats can hunt, just like their bigger, wild cousins.

Strong legs for jumping

Sharp claws

If you don't have an outdoor space, cats can be happy living indoors.

You can keep an indoor cat busy with toys and puzzles.

Most cats are happy to spend time on their own.

Cats also love to climb. An indoor climbing frame is a great way for your pet to sit high up.

Are There Different Types of Cats?

There are more than 70 different breeds, or types, of pet cats. Each breed has its own shape, fur type, colors, and markings.

Ragdoll cats are calm and gentle. They like to flop in your arms, like a real ragdoll.

A Cornish Rex cat is playful and can be easily trained.

American shorthair cat

Siamese cat

Norwegian forest cat

Persian cat

Sphynx cat

Bengal cat

A mixed-breed cat

Most pet cats are a mix of breeds, and they make perfect pets!

How Can I Make My Cat Cozy?

A cat bed

Cats spend a lot of their day sleeping.

So a pet cat should be given a soft, warm bed.

Cats can sleep for up to 18 hours a day.

A cozy box

However, your cat may curl up for a nap in the strangest of places!

A snooze in the sink

A suitcase bed

A Maine coon cat in his yard at night

Cats are most active in the early morning and late evening.

If they were wildcats, this would be their favorite time to go hunting.

When a cat wakes up, it stretches and yawns.

A scratching post helps a cat stretch its legs and keep its claws healthy and sharp.

Scratching post

What Should I Feed My Cat?

Cats are **carnivores**, and that means they only eat meat.

Cat food can be bought in pet stores and supermarkets.

These foods have all the goodness a cat needs.

Food from a can

Wet food from a pouch

Kibble is dry, crunchy, meaty food

Always feed your cat the right amount of food for its age and weight.

Your cat needs clean, fresh drinking water, too.

Place the water away from your cat's food to keep it clean.

Freshen up the water every day.

Sometimes, however, cats prefer to drink from taps and puddles!

Cats should NEVER eat these foods, as they make them sick.

- ✗ Chocolate
- ✗ Onions and garlic
- ✗ Grapes, raisins, and sultanas
- ✗ Dairy: milk, cheese, ice cream
- ✗ Raw eggs
- ✗ Raw meat or fish
- ✗ Fat trimmings
- ✗ Bones

How Clean Are Cats?

Cats are very clean. They spend lots of time licking their fur.

Tiny spines on a cat's tongue help it remove dirt from its fur.

A cat licks its paw, then rubs it around its face and ears.

Saliva on the paw cleans the fur.

Hairballs can build up in a cat's tummy if it swallows too much fur.

You can gently brush your cat to remove old fur.

An indoor cat will need a litter box filled with litter.

The cat will pee and poop in the box.

Can I Play Games with My Cat?

Yes you can! Cats love to play with their owners—even older cats.

Chasing and pouncing on toys helps a cat stay active and happy.

Remember! Our pet cats were once wild. They practice their hunting skills as they play.

Most cats love the smell of a minty plant called catnip.

Try giving your pet toys filled with dry catnip.

Cardboard boxes, tubes, crumpled paper, and ping-pong balls are all great fun to a cat!
Play games with your cat every day.
You will soon be their best friend!

When Can I Get a Kitten?

A newborn kitten has a lot of growing to do before it can leave its mother.

Mother cat

Newborn kittens

Kittens drink milk from their mom.

Kittens are born with their eyes shut and ears folded.

All kittens are born with blue eyes. They gradually change to their adult color.

After two weeks, a kitten's eyes open, and it begins to crawl.

By three weeks, its ears have unfolded, and the kitten can hear.

At eight weeks old, a kitten can eat cat food, play, wash itself, and use a litter box.

Now it is ready to live with a new owner!

How Do I Care for My New Kitten?

Before you bring your new kitten to your home, make sure you have everything it needs.

New Kitten Checklist

- Bed
- Blanket
- Collar
- Scratching post
- Litter box and litter
- Poop scoop
- Toys
- Kitten food and treats
- Bowls
- Carrier
- Brush

Always feed your kitten the right food for its age.

Kitten food has all the goodness a growing cat needs.

The kitten may be scared.
It needs time to get used to all the new sounds, smells, and people.

Show your kitten where its bed, food, and litter box are.

Don't place the litter box near your kitten's food.

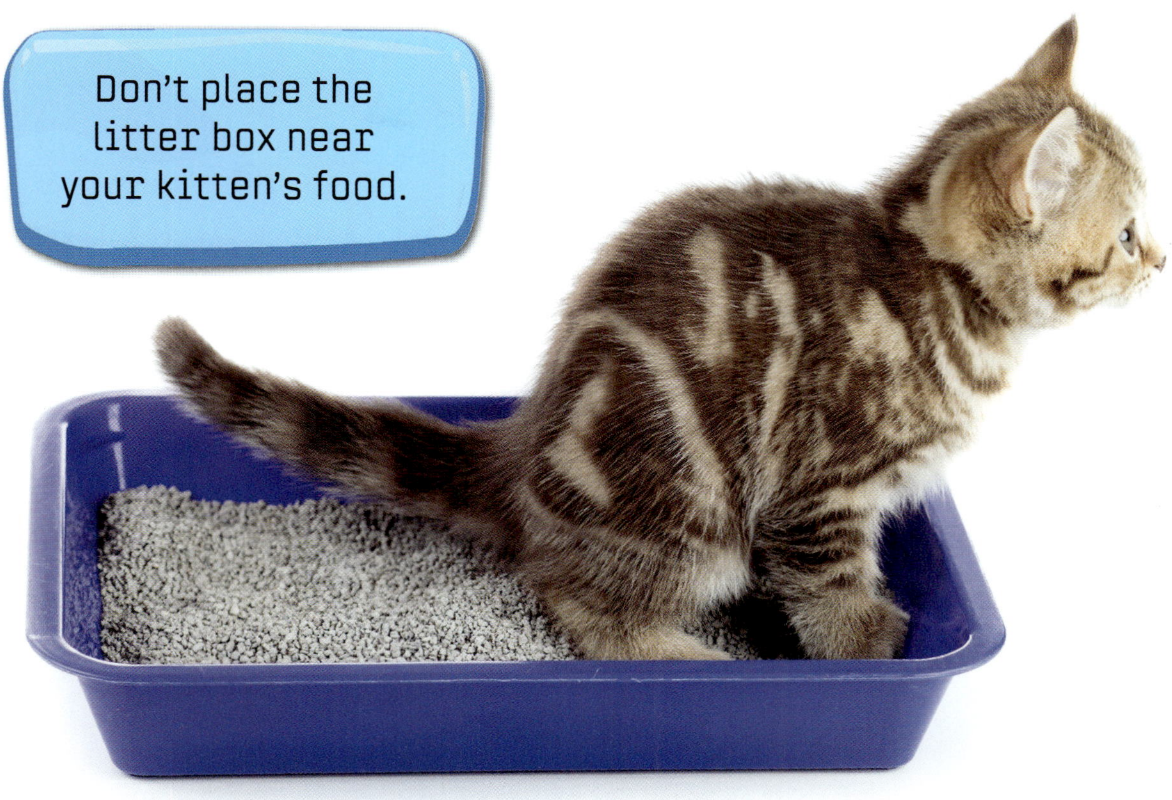

Never wake your kitten from its sleep.

Kittens need a lot of sleep because they are growing fast.

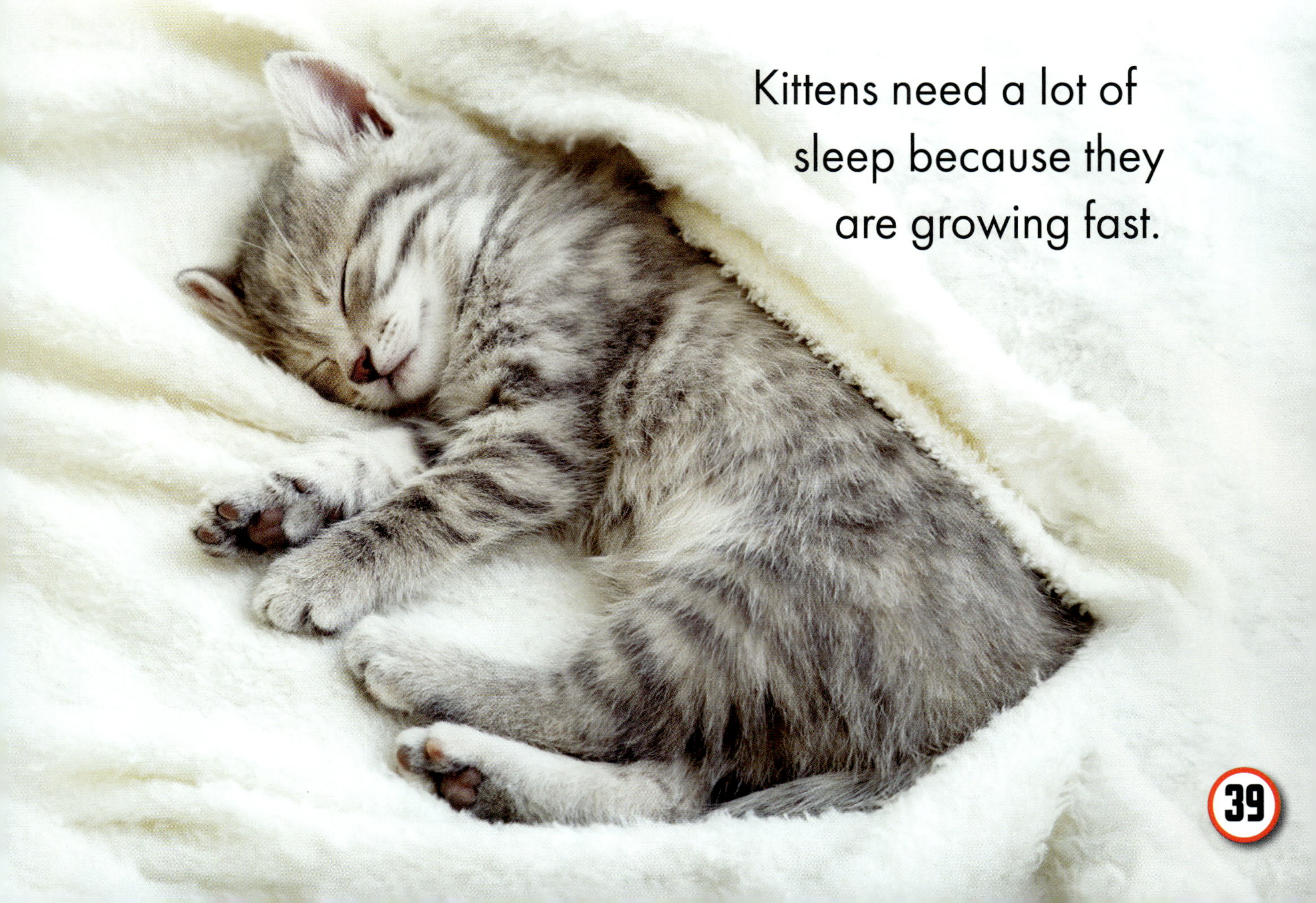

When Should My Kitten Visit the Vet?

Your new kitten should visit the vet in the first few days of coming to your home.

The vet will check your kitten's eyes, ears, tummy, and teeth.

A stethoscope helps the vet listen to your kitten's heart and lungs.

Vaccination shot

Your kitten may be given vaccinations to protect against cat diseases.

The vet will also give your kitten medicines to protect against **parasites**.

Worms are parasites that live in a pet's tummy and make it sick.

Worming medicine is put on the cat's skin.

Fleas and ticks are tiny biting parasites.

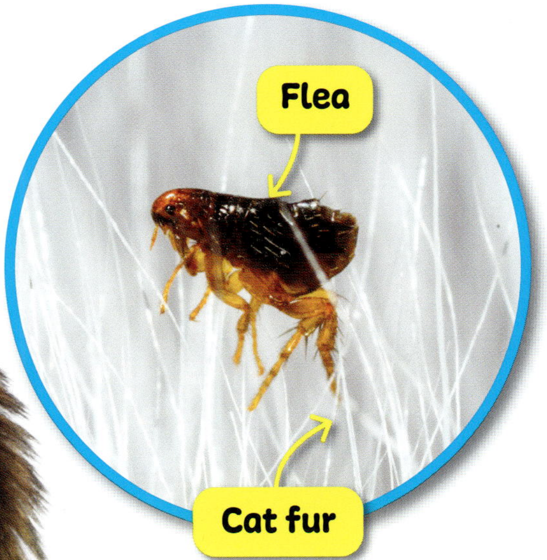

Flea

Cat fur

They can make your pet scratch and become ill.

Why Does My Cat Purr?

When cats purr, it means they are happy and comfortable.

Cats purr to say "hello" to their owners.

A short "meow" or "mew" usually means your cat is pleased to see you.

It may wind around your legs with its tail up.

When your cat is watching birds or squirrels through a window, it may chirrup and chatter.
A loud yowl may mean your cat is feeling unwell.
Cats will hiss if they are angry. They may also spit and growl.
Hiiissssssss!
Bristly tail
Arched back
Puffed-up fur
This hissing cat is saying stay away!

Do Cats Talk with Their Bodies?

Yes! You can learn how a cat is feeling by watching its body language.

A swishing tail usually means "back off!"

A scared cat crouches down low so it can quickly spring up and run.

If your cat shows its tummy, it feels safe with you.

A happy cat might knead with its paws on your lap or in another cozy spot.

Why Do We Love Dogs So Much?

Dogs are known for being our best animal friends.

They love being part of a family and being close to us.

Dogs love to share all our adventures.

Come on, Mom! Where are we going today?

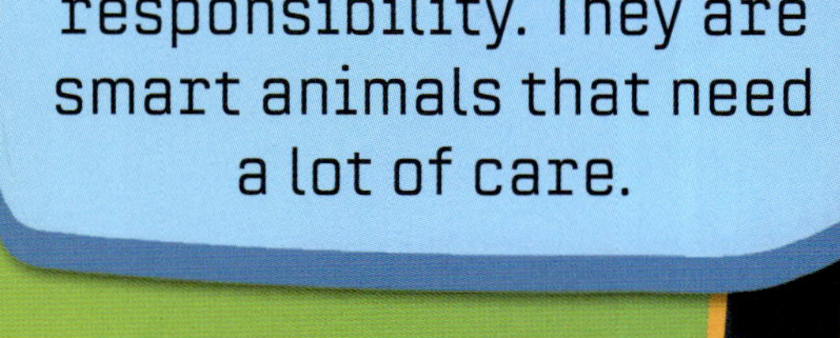

Having a dog is a big responsibility. They are smart animals that need a lot of care.

Caring for a dog means training it and helping it learn polite manners.

A well-trained dog can be taken almost anywhere.

Going on a train ride.

Dogs can be shy, fun-loving, and sometimes a little goofy!

Which Dog Is the Biggest?

Dogs come in all shapes and sizes! The biggest **breed**, or type, of dog is the Great Dane.

There are more than 350 breeds of dogs.

Many dogs are a mix of two or more different breeds.

Poodle

King Charles Cavalier Spaniel

Golden Retriever

All dogs have a powerful sense of smell.

Sniffing is their way of finding out about the world.

Could I Give a Dog a Home?

Getting a dog is a big decision. You must find out all about the things your dog will need.

Questions to Ask Before Getting a Dog

- Do we have time to care for a dog?
- Is there enough space?
- Who can help out when we are away?
- How much exercise will the dog need?
- How much will the dog cost?
- Who will help feed, exercise, and train the dog?

Don't forget we must pick up our dog's poop, too!

Most dogs need a yard to play and relax.

Dogs need to be around people and other pets. They shouldn't be left alone for hours at a time.

What Does My Dog Need?

Your new dog will be coming home soon!

New Dog Checklist

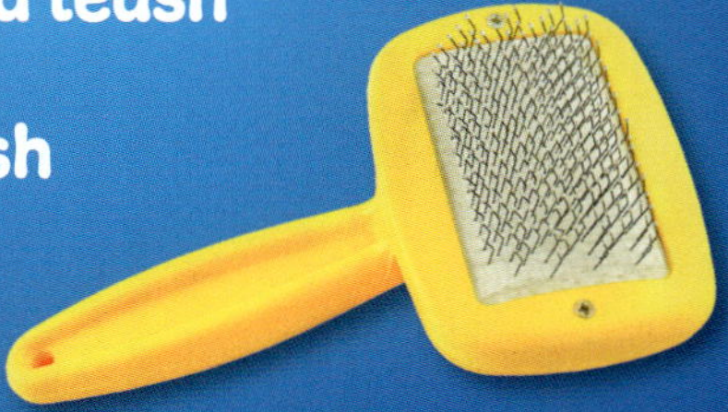

- Bed and blanket
- Bowls
- Poop bags
- Toys
- Collar and leash
- Brush

Find a veterinary clinic for your dog before it comes home.

Dogs like to chew.

Make sure you have plenty of chew toys for your new pet.

The yard must be safe. Make sure your dog can't escape.

Your dog must wear a special tag on its collar, in case it gets lost or runs off.

Collar identification tag

The identification tag has your address and telephone number on it.

What Do Dogs Eat?

Dogs are **omnivores**. This means they can eat meat, fish, and some fruits and vegetables.

However, some foods can make dogs sick.

Dangerous Foods for Dogs

- ✗ Onions and garlic
- ✗ Grapes, raisins, and sultanas
- ✗ Nuts
- ✗ Chocolate
- ✗ Avocados
- ✗ Coffee
- ✗ Milk, cheese, and yogurt
- ✗ Human cakes and cookies

Dog food from a supermarket or pet store has all the goodness a dog needs.

Wet food is soft and meaty.

Kibble is dry, crunchy, meaty biscuits.

Always feed your dog the right food for its age.

A Labrador puppy

An old Labrador dog

Food for growing pups has extra energy.

Never feed your dog too much. It might get too heavy and become unhealthy.

Make sure your dog always has fresh drinking water.

What Does My Dog Like to Do?

Dogs love to be active. They enjoy walking, swimming, digging, and playing games.

Most dogs have strong jaws, so they love a game of tug.

Try training your dog to fetch by throwing a ball.

Each time your dog brings the ball back to you, reward it with a tiny food treat.

Let your puppy explore and sniff out new smells on a walk.

Put treats into a doggie puzzle toy to keep your dog's mind happy and active.

When Can a New Pup Come Live with Me?

When a puppy is born, it needs its mom for food, warmth, and love.

After about 10 days, a puppy's eyes begin to open. At three weeks old, it can hear.

Three-week-old puppy

Four-week-old puppy

At four weeks old, a puppy can sit up and take its first steps.

At six weeks, a puppy loves to play, wag its tail, and bark.

At eight weeks old, a growing pup is usually ready to leave its mom and meet its new owner!

Eight-week-old puppy

Will My New Puppy Be Scared?

Everything in your home will be new to your puppy.

Give it time to explore and get used to all the new sounds and smells.

The TV, washing machine, and vacuum can be loud!

Slowly introduce your puppy to your other pets.

Give them time to get to know your puppy, too.

Get your pup used to car rides. Speak softly to the puppy to **reassure** it.

Puppies need vaccinations before they can safely walk on the ground outdoors.

Let your pup see the outside world by taking it for walks in a stroller.

What Happens When My Puppy Visits the Vet?

The vet will check your puppy's eyes, ears, teeth, breathing, and weight.

The vet will give your puppy vaccination shots.

The vet may also give your puppy medicine to protect it from fleas, ticks, and worms.

The vet can inject a tiny microchip with a special number into your puppy or kitten.

The microchip is just the size of a grain of rice and won't hurt your pet.

If the animal gets lost and found, a vet can read the number with a scanner.

The number tells the vet where your pet lives.

Lost puppy

Scanner

What's In a Bark?

Dogs make different noises to communicate with us and each other.

When someone knocks at the door, a dog may give a deep bark.

This is a warning to strangers to stay away.

A high-pitched bark means your dog is excited!

A whine can mean your dog is scared.

I don't like fireworks, Dad!

When a dog growls, it is saying, "I'm not happy. Back off!"

Wolves howl to communicate over long distances.

Pet dogs may howl, too, especially if they hear sirens or certain music.

Why Do Dogs Wag Their Tails?

Your dog uses its body to communicate with you and other dogs.

Happy Dog

A wagging tail is a dog's way of saying, "Hi."

Scared Dog

This dog is saying, "I'm frightened."

Playful Dog

If a dog wants to play, it does a play bow with its bottom in the air!

Be Safe Around Dogs

Never touch or go up to a strange dog.

Even gentle dogs may not like being touched by strangers.

Always ask an owner if you can pet their dog.

The dog will lose interest in you.

If a strange dog comes up to you, stay very still and look away.

How Do I Care for a Rabbit?

Rabbits need careful care. They must always live with other rabbits to feel happy.

Rabbits love to dig, **burrow**, hop, and jump, so give them plenty of space.

They need a safe, warm, quiet place where they can rest.

A rabbit digging in its yard

Rabbits make good house pets and will enjoy being part of the family.

What Do Rabbits Eat?

Their main food is fresh hay.

Hay

Rabbit pellets

Leafy greens such as kale, salad leaves, and watercress

Carrot tops

They need fresh food and water every day.

Rabbits love to chew! Give them cardboard tubes, dried apple sticks, and special rabbit toys to chew.

Rabbit chew toy

Why Do Guinea Pigs Squeak?

Guinea pigs are small rodents that like to live in groups.

They squeak to communicate with each other.

Guinea pigs need other guinea pigs! Never keep one alone.

What Do Guinea Pigs Eat?

Hay and grass

They need fresh hay, grass, guinea pig pellets, vegetables, and fresh water every day.

Cucumber

Kale

Bell peppers

Celery

Parsley

Guinea pigs need a safe **enclosure** with room to explore and play.

An outdoor summer enclosure

Who Stuffs Their Cheeks with Food?

Hamsters have cheek pouches that they stuff with food.

This is how wild hamsters carry food back to their burrows.

Pet hamsters like to live alone. They also like to dig and burrow.

Hamsters need lots of deep bedding for burrowing.

Bedding

Gerbils are happy living in pairs.

Buy food for your hamster or gerbils from the pet store.

How Smart Is a Rat?

Pet rats are super smart! They like to live in pairs.

Rats love spending time with their owners and can even learn simple tricks.

Give pet rats toys and cardboard boxes and tubes to explore.

This keeps their smart brains busy.

Pet mice can be kept in pairs and small groups.

They love to make cozy nests, so give them plenty of nesting material.

You can build a mouse adventure playground!

Toilet paper tube

Pet mouse

Always buy special rat and mouse food from a pet store.

Which Pets Sing, Whistle, and Talk?

Colorful, friendly pet birds do!

Canaries love to sing.

Canary

You can buy special seeds for your birds to eat from a pet store.

Cockatiels talk to their owners with whistles.

Parakeet

Cockatiel

Parakeets can learn to talk!

A pet bird may live for up to 15 years. It needs lots of care for many years.

Choose a cage with space for pet birds to stretch their wings and flutter around.

Allow pet birds plenty of time outside of their cage, too.

Do Pet Birds Take Baths?

Yes, they do! Bathing removes dead skin and loose feathers.

Shallow dish of room-temperature water

Canary bathing

Being wet helps a bird clean its feathers with its beak.

Parakeets can copy what you say!

Start by saying, "Hello," or your bird's name, again and again.

Chopped veggies

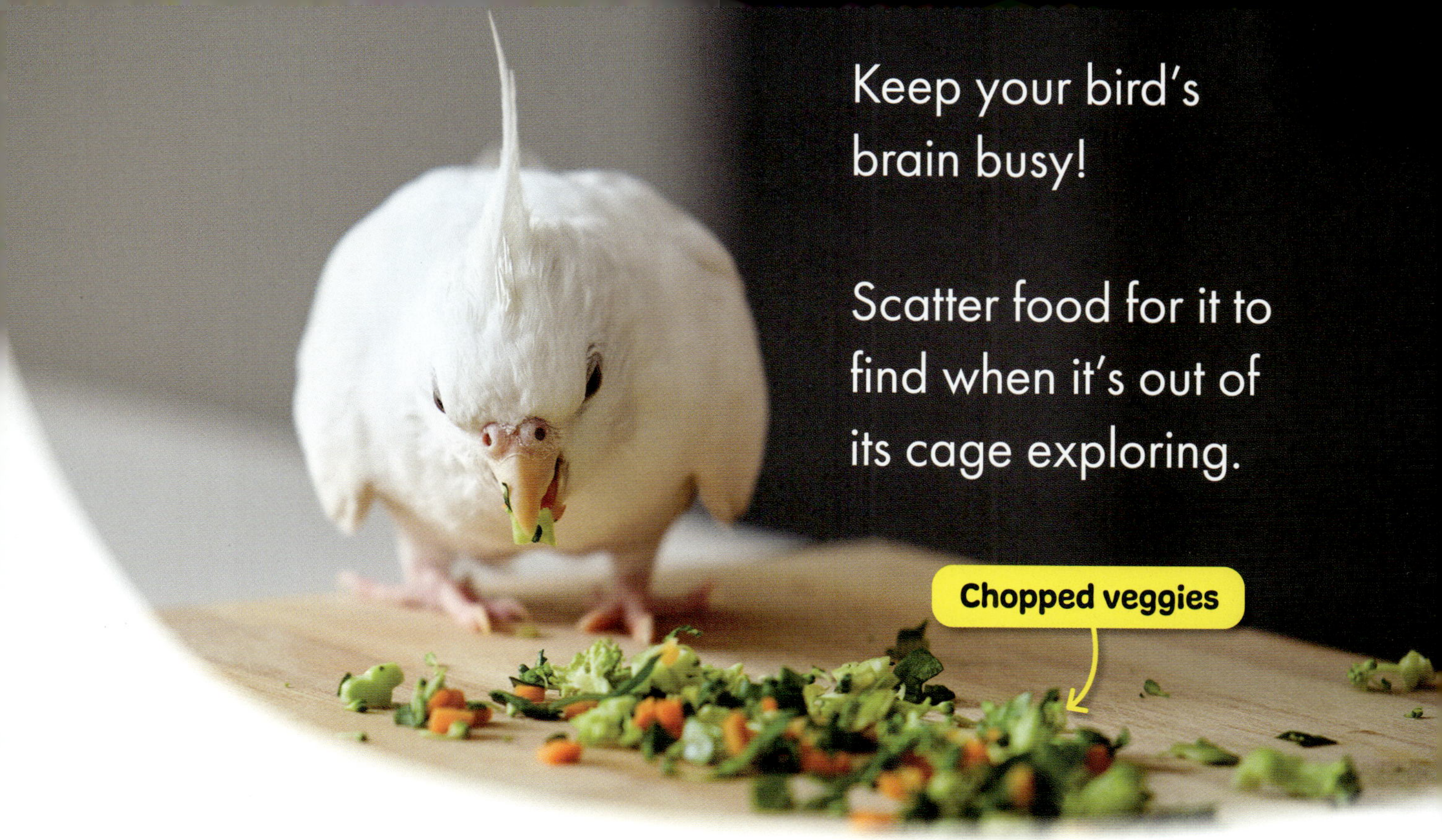

Keep your bird's brain busy!

Scatter food for it to find when it's out of its cage exploring.

Pet birds sleep at night, just like humans do.

They need darkness and quiet, so try covering your bird's cage.

Sleeping parakeet

Pet birds need up to 12 hours of sleep each night.
Ssshhh
Zzzzzzz

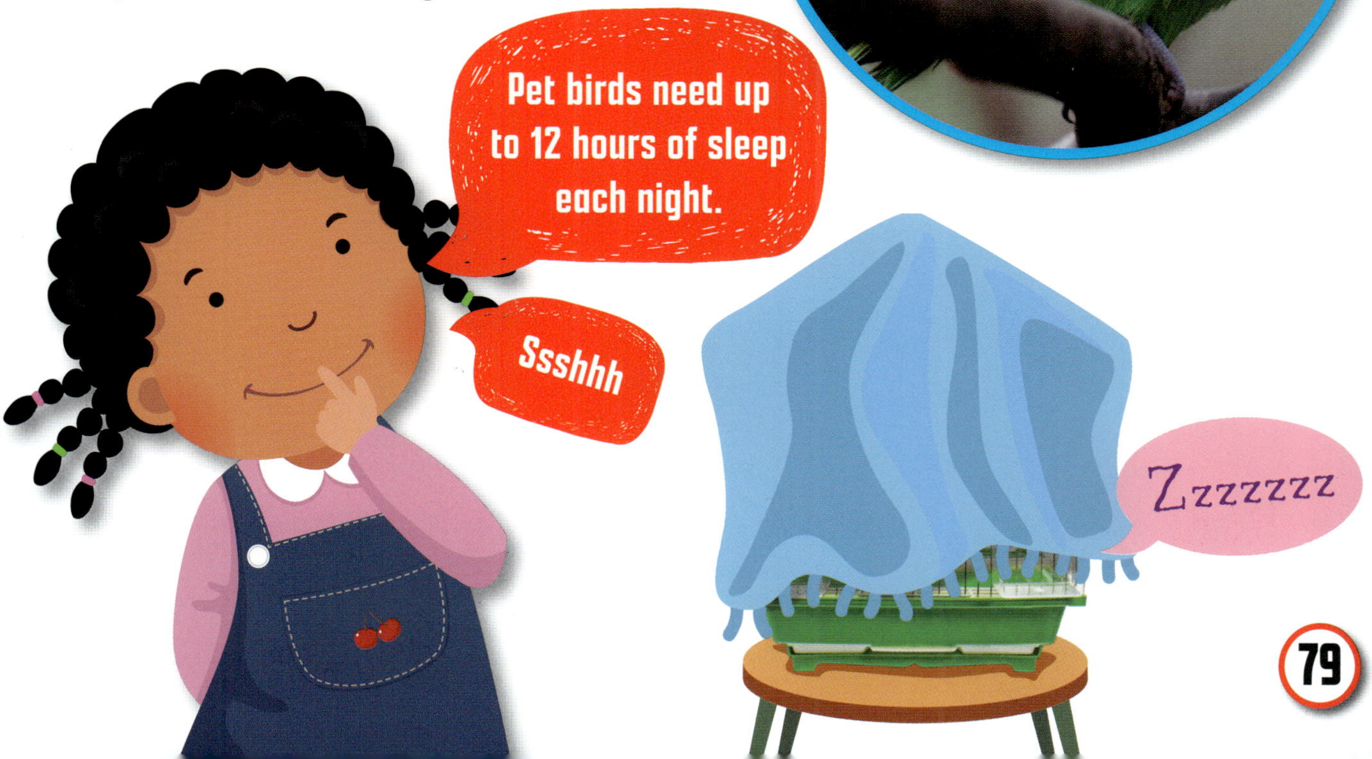

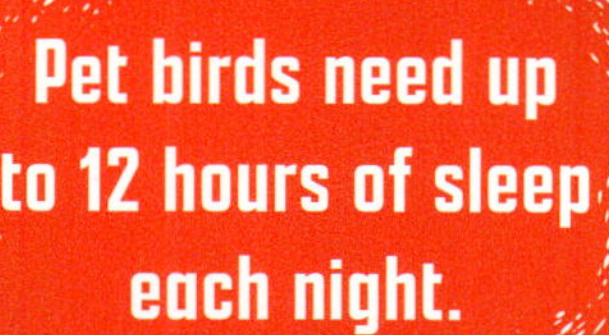

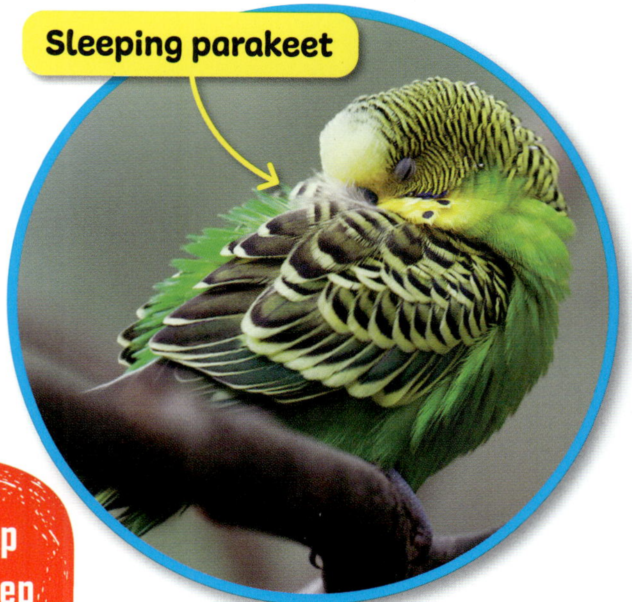

How Do I Care for Tropical Fish?

You must make sure that your pet fish have everything they need in their tank called an aquarium.

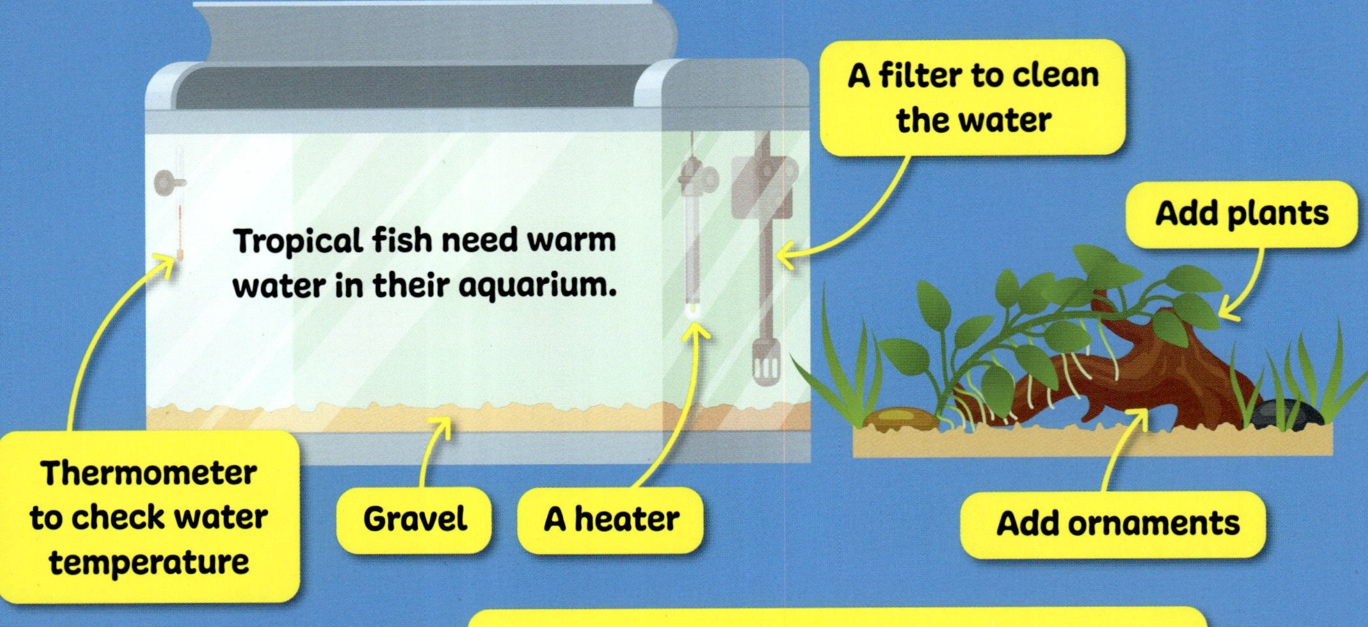

Tetras, mollies, and guppies are good tropical fish to have as first pets.

They are easier to care for.

Tetra

Molly

Guppy

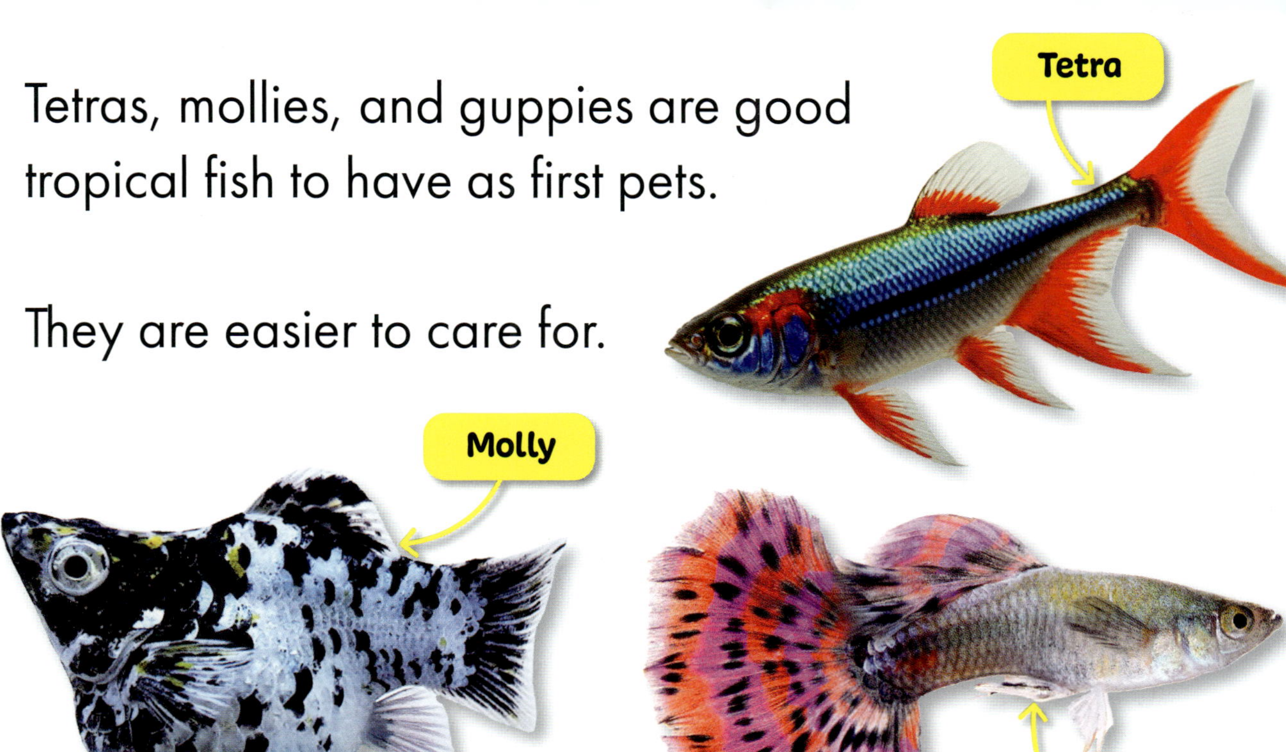

Your fish will swim through and hide in the ornaments.

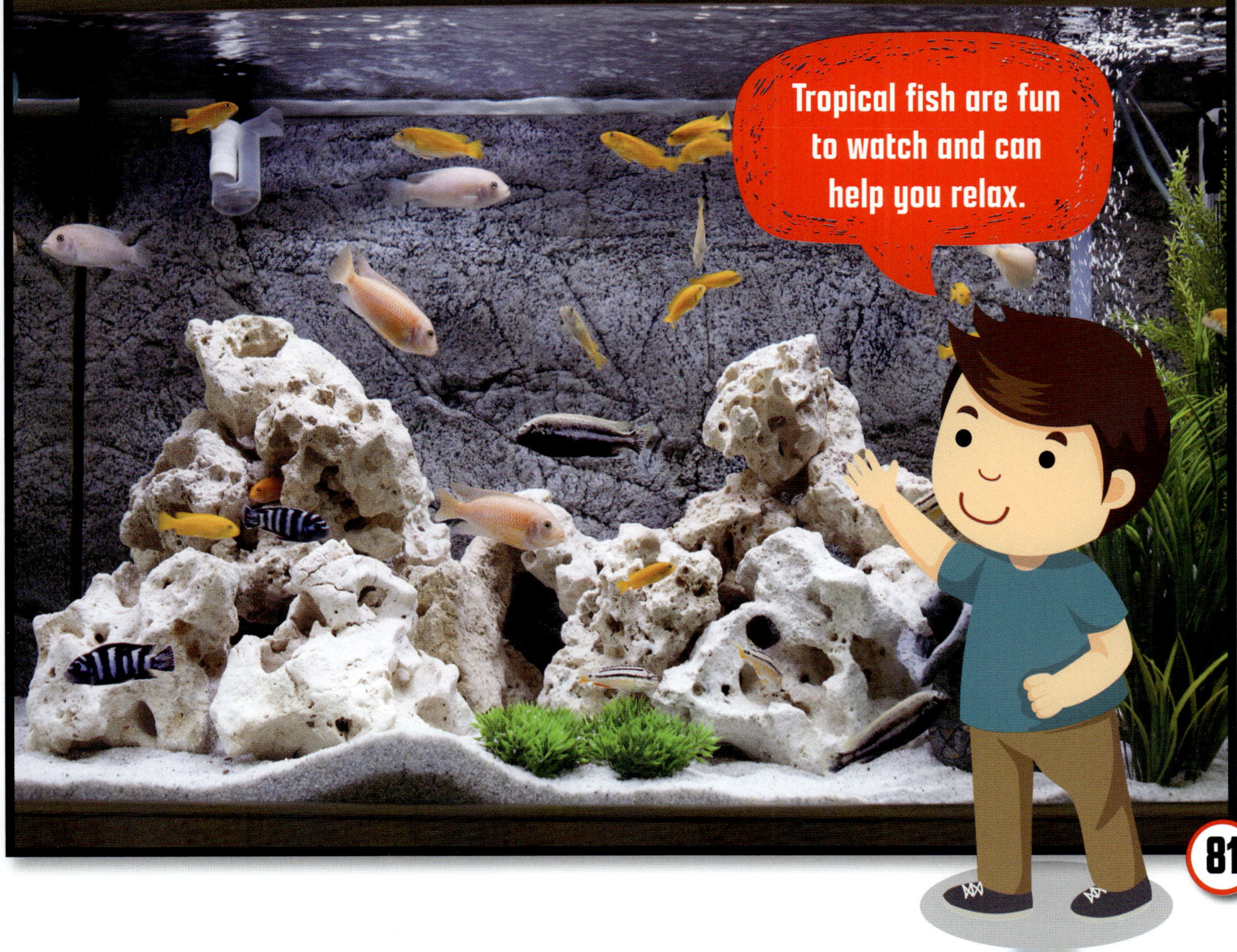

Tropical fish are fun to watch and can help you relax.

Can I Be Friends with a Fish?

Pet goldfish are fascinating pets. Take good care of them, and you will become their best friend.

Keep goldfish in small groups in an aquarium tank.

Goldfish are coldwater fish that like cool water in their tanks.

Never keep goldfish in a small bowl!

A healthy goldfish can live for up to 15 years.

Goldfish

Add water plants to the aquarium for your goldfish to nibble on.

Anubias
Java moss

Elodea

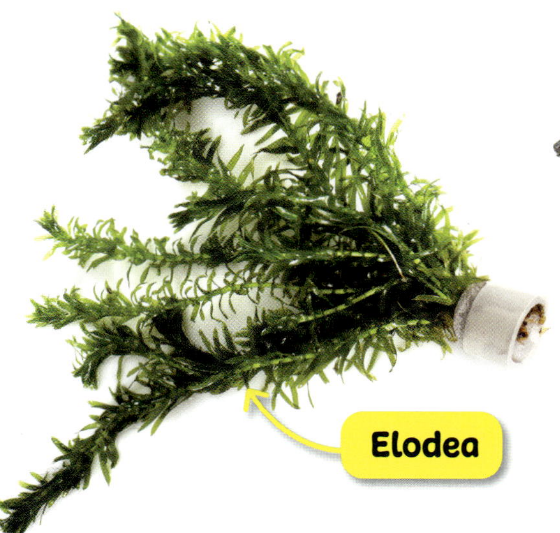

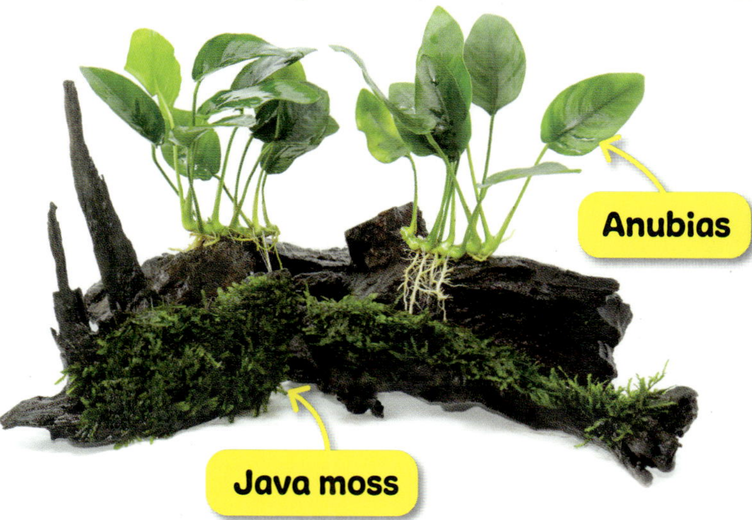

Don't overfeed goldfish or they will become overweight.

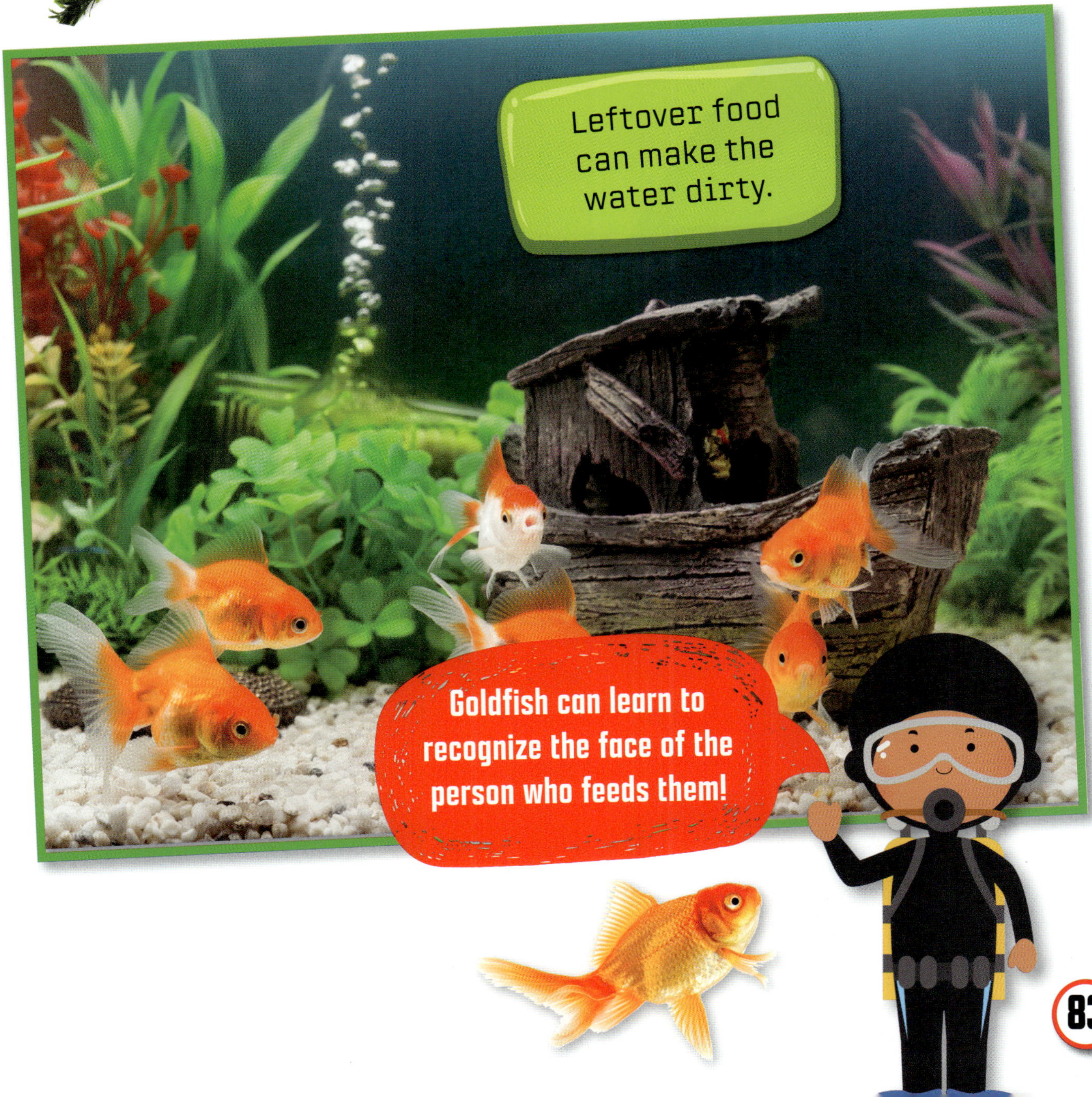
Leftover food can make the water dirty.
Goldfish can learn to recognize the face of the person who feeds them!

How Long Does a Tortoise Live?

Tortoises are **reptiles**. Some kinds can live for up to 100 years!

Hard shell

Beaky mouth for biting plants

Scaly legs

Only tortoises born in **captivity** can be sold as pets. Wild tortoises cannot be captured.

Try not to handle a pet tortoise unless it needs help. Just watch and enjoy!

A tortoise needs an outdoor enclosure with sunny spots, shade, and a shelter.

Top Tortoise Foods

Chicory

Dandelions

Clover

Timothy grass

You can grow chicory, lamb's lettuce, and grasses for your tortoise.

Lamb's lettuce

Can I Keep a Snake as a Pet?

Snakes are reptiles. Some kinds can be pets.

A corn snake can be gently handled.

Scaly skin

Corn snakes that are bred in captivity are good starter snakes.

Vivarium

Snakes need to live in a special heated tank called a vivarium.

Snakes are carnivores. Owners buy dead mice and rats from pet stores to feed their snakes.

Corn snake

Tongue

Snakes flick their tongues in and out to pick up smells, such as food.

Snakes shed their outer layer of skin three or four times a year.

This keeps their skin healthy and free from parasites.

Rat snake

New fresh skin

Old skin

Can I Have a Pet Dragon?

You can if it's a bearded dragon!

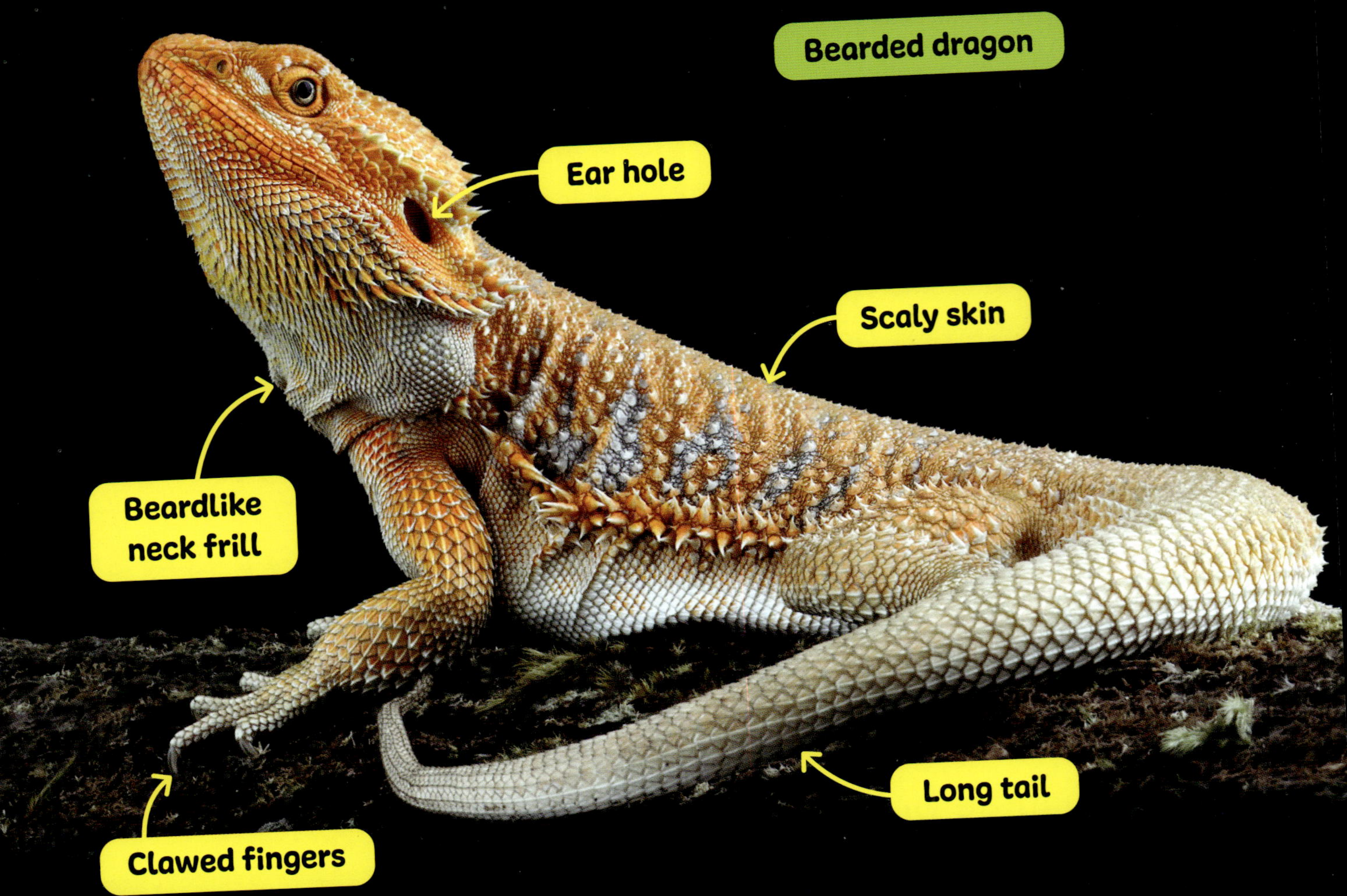

Bearded dragon
Ear hole
Scaly skin
Beardlike neck frill
Long tail
Clawed fingers

Bearded dragons are omnivores that eat insects and plants.

They use their long tongue to grab insects, such as crickets.

Cricket
Tweezers

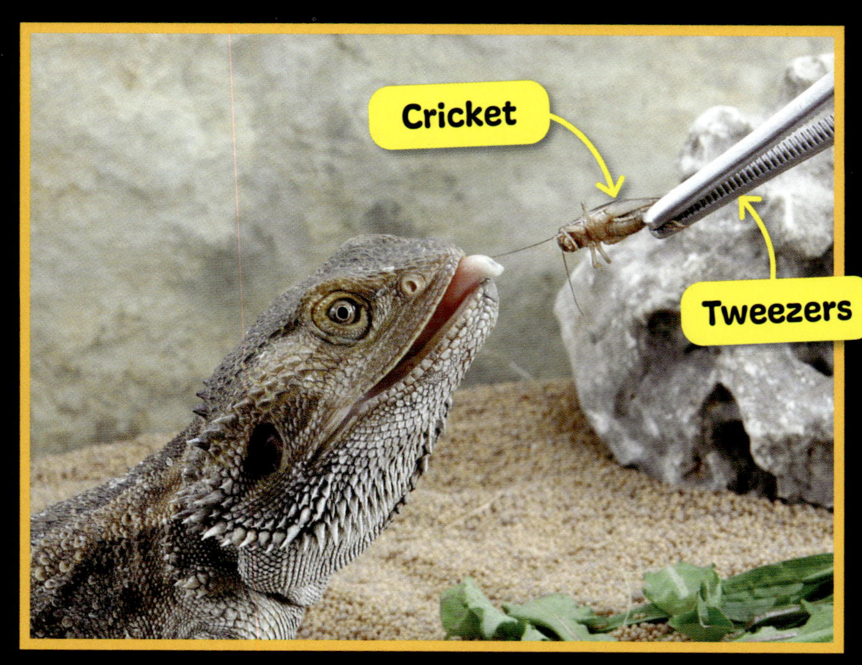

A bearded dragon's tank should be warm with a place to sleep.

There should also be rocks and branches because they like to climb.

Bearded dragons wave and bob their heads to communicate with each other and their owners.

Your dragon can leave its home to explore if it's in a warm, safe place.

Which Pets Have Clever Disguises?

Stick insects and leaf insects are disguised as twigs and leaves.

These pets are delicate and should be handled very gently.

Stick insects eat plants and love munching on the leaves of brambles, ivy, and privet.

Stick insects also love to climb.

A stick insect needs a tall enclosure with lots of leaves.

Leaf insects have wings, but they are poor fliers.

They sometimes try to glide!

In the wild, a leaf insect's disguise helps it hide from hungry birds and other **predators**.

Perfect Pet Facts

Rabbits have soft and hard poop. They eat their own soft poop to get an extra dose of goodness!

Rats pee a lot. They send messages to other rats with their pee.

A baby rabbit is called a kitten. Kittens are born blind and have no fur.

Unlike a human, a cat can see in the dark. Having super nighttime vision helps their wild cousins hunt at night.

Wild guinea pigs are called cavies. They live in groups of up to 20 animals.

Pet dogs can understand over 100 words and commands. The smartest dog breed is the Border Collie.

Border Collie

Bearded dragons are lizards that lay eggs from which their babies hatch.

Alpacas and llamas will spit if they are scared or annoyed.

Tortoises have been around for millions of years. They lived alongside the dinosaurs!

Llamas are very good at guarding. They will keep animals like sheep, chickens, and ducks safe from predators such as foxes.

A female mouse can have a litter of up to 10 babies every six weeks!

Hamsters love to run. Wild hamsters may travel up to 5 miles (8 km) each night.

When pet cats died in ancient Egypt, they were made into mummies and buried with their owners.

Cat mummy

The world's longest insect is a type of stick insect. It can grow to 2 feet (61 cm) long!

My Pet Words

ancient Egyptians
A group of people who lived in Egypt in Africa thousands of years ago.

animal sanctuary
A safe place where animals, such as unwanted pets or farm animals, can have a forever home. Wild animals that have been hurt may also live in a sanctuary.

animal shelter
A place where unwanted pets are cared for. The workers at a shelter find the pets forever homes by matching them with new owners.

body language
Using body parts or your face to communicate. When you smile, you show people you are happy without saying the words.

breed
A group of animals raised by humans that look alike and have similar personalities. For example, a Golden Retriever is a breed of dog.

burrow
To dig into the ground to make a tunnel or underground home.

captivity
Having parents that did not live as wild animals, but lived as pets, on a farm, or in a zoo.

carnivore
An animal that only eats meat.

communicate
To share information and feelings by making sounds or using body language.

content
Feeling happy, calm, comfortable, and safe.

enclosure
A safe caged or fenced place where a pet, farm, or zoo animal lives.

omnivore
An animal that eats meat and plants.

parasite
A small animal that lives on or in another animal called the host. Parasites feed on their hosts and can make them sick.

predator
An animal that hunts and eats other animals.

reassure
To make an animal or another person feel safe. You might reassure a pet by quietly talking to it or gently stroking it.

reptile
An animal with scaly skin, such as a snake or lizard. Reptiles are cold-blooded, which means they cannot keep their bodies warm without sunlight or a heater.

responsible
Taking care of something and remembering important things you must do, such as feeding a pet.

rodent
Small, furry animals such as mice, rats, and hamsters. Rodents' teeth are always growing, so they like to chew and gnaw on things.

tamed
No longer being wild. A tamed animal may be gentle, calm, and easy to train.

Big Pets Quiz

1: Which of these pets is a relative of wolves?
a] Guinea pig
b] Pony
c] Dog

2: Where is the best place to find a new pet?
a] A pet store
b] An animal shelter
c] A farm

3: Who helps make sick pets better?
a] A vet
b] A doctor
c] A dentist

4: Which of these pets is a carnivore?
a] A stick insect
b] A hamster
c] A cat

5: Which breed of dog is the biggest?
a] Chihuahua
b] Great Dane
c] Labrador

6: At what age can a puppy leave its mother?
a] Eight months
b] Eight days
c] Eight weeks

7: Which of these pets is a rodent?
a] A guinea pig
b] A rabbit
c] A goldfish

8: What pet can learn to say words?
a] A rat
b] A rabbit
c] A parakeet

9: What does a dog's wagging tail mean?
a] I'm happy
b] I'm scared
c] I feel sick

10: What pet might live in a vivarium?
a] A snake
b] A fish
c] A tortoise

Answers:
1] c 2] b 3] a 4] c 5] b 6] c
7] a 8] c 9] a 10] a